CW01501657

DIY Natural

Pour Soap Crafting

Ultimate Guide to Making & Selling Colorful Natural Soaps

(Recipes Included)

BY

Molly Barrett

CSB Academy Publishing Co.

P. O. Box 966

Semmes, Alabama 36575, USA

Cover Design & Layout

By

Robin Hamilton

First Edition

CONTENTS IN THIS BOOK

INTRODUCTION

It started out innocently enough with a simple question: "You made this soap yourself?"

"I wish *I* could do something like this," I said, sighing with jealousy. My friend assured me I could.

She had just given me a gift of several bars of homemade, gloriously decorated soap. For the longest time, I refused to use them. They were obviously too beautiful. Once I did, though, I fell in love with the way they made my body feel.

It started on a small scale. I called her to see if I could just watch her make a batch of soap. She welcomed me and encouraged me. I was amazed at how easy it looked.

The next thing I knew I was making soap myself. And not only did I enjoy doing it, but the end product, *my* end product looked pretty darned good.

My interest grew. Soon I was making gifts for everyone from my grandmother to my mother, my friends, and co-workers. People sincerely loved them, and before I knew it, they were in my kitchen asking me to teach them to make their own soap.

While I was busy making soap for gifts, my husband sat me down and asked me to read an article he found in one of those health magazines you get at local health food stores. It talked about the dangers in commercially manufactured soap. It seems that many of the additives used in these products are potentially dangerous.

That certainly gave me a unique perspective on my new-found hobby.

That's when the entire situation exploded – in a good way, that is. I started a small business, selling at local craft shows, then I expanded to the web, on Etsy, the ultimate online craft store, and eBay.

And that's how this book was born. My friends requested I write a how-to book on soap making at its most basic level. A book for beginners, who have no knowledge about the subject, could read, use, and successfully make soap.

How the Chapters are Arranged

So, I finally relented. In creating the guidebook, I wanted to arrange the chapters in a logical order. I thought back to my first days and my confusion over how to make the soap, the terms, and the many health benefits.

That's why, even before we begin to talk about the process itself, I talk a bit about my family. I explain, why now, we use nothing but homemade soap in our house. The article my husband asked me to read stuck in my mind like a bad earworm. I couldn't imagine going back to using commercial soap after that.

And it bothered me so much that I continued to research it on the web.

If only half of what I read about the dangers of the additives in these soaps are true, then it's no surprise that so many people have unexplained health ailments. Many times these issues aren't severe enough to see a healthcare provider about, but just bad enough that your body tells you something is wrong. I talk about only three of these (in Chapter 1) just to give you a small glimpse into the world of commercially made soap.

Once I put the additives in perspective, I decided it was in my best interest as well as the interests of my family to do even more research on soap making. But, I learned the more I read about soap making, the more confused I became.

What especially confused me were the different processes that were used. At first, I wasn't even aware there was any process other than the simple melt-and-pour method. But there are two more: cold-process and hot-process. I distinguish these as quickly as possible (Chapter 2) so as you do your own research, you experience a little less confusion than I did.

By the time you've read the first two chapters, you're probably getting somewhat impatient, itchy to make your own soap and enjoy the results. But before we begin detailing the rudimentary instructions, it's wise to know what you'll need when it comes to your basic equipment and supplies (Chapter 3), next I guide you through a step-by-step soap making process (chapter 4). Naturally, the molds come next in chapter 5. And, yes, it is all about molds and all their variations and types.

After that we discuss colors (chapter 6) and essential oils that give your soap its scent and healing power (Chapter 7). After that it is all about my favorite recipes (chapter 8). Then I share 15 soap coloring tricks that may truly surprise you. Yes, they are really that good (chapter 9).

It's best to have these items lined up before you even begin to work on your first project. I found out the hard way that if you run short of the type of soap you need, you simply can't knock on your neighbor's door for a cup of lye (a soap making ingredient) like you would for a cup of sugar for a dessert recipe.

After you've read this far and undoubtedly have at least a few projects under your belt, you may be thinking about taking that step of starting your own soap-making business. In case your mind keeps returning to this possibility, I've written a bit about how to organize yourself, a bit on marketing and even some of the obstacles you may run into along the way (Chapter 10).

But first things first. I can't tell you my outrage about discovering a number of potentially dangerous additives and how wide-spread their use is in just about every commercially made cosmetic in this country. Let's get started.

CHAPTER 1: WHAT'S IN YOUR SOAP?

4 HARMFUL CHEMICAL IN YOUR SOAP

PARABENS. SULFATES. TRICLOSANS

These are some of the ingredients in commercial soap that I never questioned until I began making it at home. That's when my curiosity got the best of me.

After finding just these three, I wanted to call a truce to look for dangerous additives in what I used (and worse yet, my children used) to clean.

That's when I thought I found the fourth one. Fragrance! How in the world could something that sounds as harmless as fragrance possibly damage your skin? How wrong I was. The definition of "fragrance" is a far cry from what it actually is on the soap label.

I began making soap because it was a fun hobby I could share with my children. I continued because it morphed into a successful small business. But I'm now compelled to continue knowing that I'm contributing to the health of my family.

Before we get into the actual soap making, I'd like to share with you my findings about these four potentially harmful ingredients found in too many soaps and body washes.

You may be wondering how something, when applied to your skin, can cause harm to your organs. Good question. What I hadn't remembered from elementary school science was that the skin is the largest organ of your body. On average it's approximately 22 square feet.

Let that number soak in for a moment. That's the amount of potential skin available for harmful additives to seep into your body.

While most of the nutrients we receive in order to enjoy good health are swallowed, your body also absorbs nutrients through the skin. In fact, roughly 60 percent of everything you put on your skin eventually gets absorbed and finds its way to the bloodstream.

And the skin is indiscriminate about what it absorbs. You place something on your skin and it will eventually lap it up. Of course, it soaks up vitamins and minerals you feed it. But it'll will also absorb all sorts of harmful additives, such as parabens, sulfates and Triclosans. And yes, the four additives I've already mentioned do eventually find their way into your bloodstream. And they are potentially very harmful. Below is a quick rundown on what they do once they're in your body.

Parabens

Scientists refer to this substance as an estrogen mimicker. That means that when the parabens do enter your bloodstream, your body mistakenly identifies them as the hormone estrogen. Because of that, parabens have also been called "hormone disruptors."

The body, believing that there is too much estrogen in its bloodstream, tries to get rid of it. This can occur any number of ways. Your body can decrease your body muscle mass, increase fat deposits or even cause reproductive problems in both men and women. It's also believed that parabens are known to be at least partially responsible for the early onset of puberty in children.

Sulfates

These chemicals are in commercially sold soap. Its primary job is to produce the lather and bubbles we've come to love. If you look at the labels of the soaps and body washes these are normally identified as SLS or sodium lauryl sulfate and SLES known as sodium laureth sulfates.

Lather and bubbles are good things to have in soap, though, aren't they?

Well, of course, they are but at what cost? These chemicals increase the penetration of the skin's surface and deplete your skin of its natural oils. If you suffer from sensitive or dry skin or eczema, sulfates only make a possible bad situation even worse.

Triclosan

You'll find this dangerous additive most often in antibacterial soap. Recently, studies have been conducted on this ingredient producing some worrisome results. Soaps that use triclosan are actually not killing bacteria, instead they encourage the growth of antibiotic-resistant bacteria.

If that weren't enough triclosan also creates a carcinogen known as **dioxin**, which has been found in high levels in breast milk.

Dioxins, like parabens, are hormone disruptors and can affect, specifically, the functioning of your thyroid. Even more problematic than that, though, is the fact that this is a carcinogen, a potential cancer-causing substance.

The Deceptive Term: Fragrance

When I first saw the word "fragrance" on the commercially made soap, I finally felt I found an additive that isn't harmful. Then I learned that the word is referred to the scent of the product, as I thought. But, then I learned that there was nothing natural about this word.

In fact, when you see this term on soap, more than likely it refers to a "cocktail" of chemicals. What chemicals exactly? You'll never discover them from reading the label. The FDA doesn't mandate soap producers to disclose the analysis of the **"fragrance."** Why? Because these lists of chemicals are considered to be propriety property – or in plain language, "trade secrets."

There's only one problem with this. The only party that is kept in the dark about the contents of these blends are the consumers. The competition can easily discover the ingredients of the cocktails by taking the product to a chemist who can analyze the ingredients as well as the proportions of these ingredients. So much for trade secrets.

There are, however, a few things we know for sure. One of the chemicals most commonly used are a class of chemicals called **"phthalates."** These are used to make fragrances last longer, but in addition to being synthetically made, they have already been identified as carcinogens, cancer-causing chemicals.

Scientific studies have already revealed that constant exposure to fragrances are also responsible for adversely affecting the central nervous system. Additionally, the ingredients in the fragrances have been known to trigger allergies, migraine headaches as well as the symptoms of asthma.

You may be wondering what else commercial soap is doing to not only your skin but your entire system as well. Below I've gathered a list of disorders and other health concerns that have been associated with additives used in many common commercially made soaps.

- Shortness of breath
- Tightness in the chest
- Dizziness
- Fatigue
- Migraine headaches
- Nausea
- Sinus conditions
- Hives

- Unexplained rashes
- Dermatitis
- Sore throat
- Cough
- Unexplained irritations to the mouth, eyes, skin, and lungs

I started making soap as a creative outlet and a method to give cute small gifts, usually on the spur of the moment. I continued making soap when I realized that I could make an income selling them. But now I will probably never stop making it after discovering the dangers of commercial soap. It is now a necessity and not a hobby or a luxury.

In the next chapter, I'll show you just what it takes, in terms of equipment, supplies and financial investment to get you started on a recreational level.

CHAPTER 2: HOT? COLD? MELT AND POUR? THREE METHODS OF SOAP-MAKING

LYE. GLYCERIN.

I can tell from your vocabulary, you've been scouring the web reading up on soap making. You'd really like to give it a try, but . . .

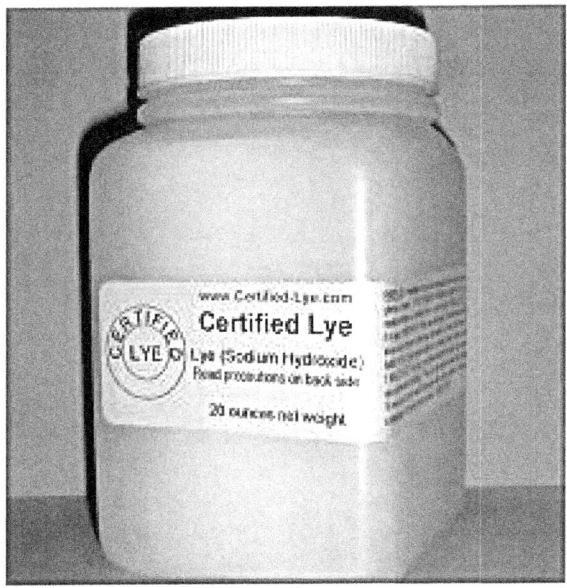

You don't know where to start. You got lost in the jungle of terms soap makers use with little or no explanation. You're not alone. Most people do. And unfortunately, too many of them abandon their idea and miss out on one of the most satisfying hobbies anyone could adopt.

It's time to explain these terms, so they aren't intimidating and explain the differences among the three methods of soap making.

This guide shows you how to make the melt-and-pour method. This technique is often called the "easiest" of your three choices and is sometimes shunned by those who use either the "cold" or "hot" processes.

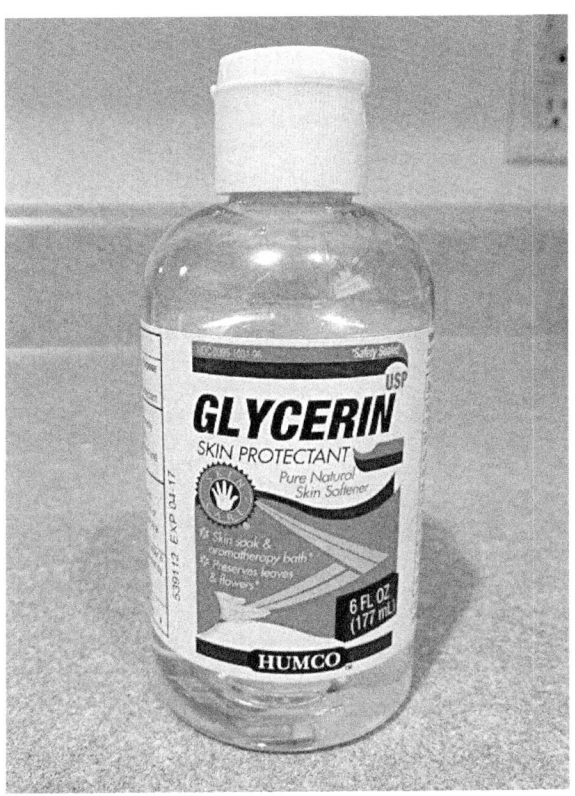

Before your eyes glaze over wondering about those three processes in one paragraph, you need to know I'm about to explain all three methods. And I promise not to explain them all in the same paragraph

 In this book, I'm only going to teach you the melt-and-pour method. You may wonder why just melt and pour. This is best and easiest method for making most soaps, this is the method 95% of the home based soap makers use and lastly, yes, I too use this method, and only this method in all of my own soap makings.

First, let's dispel the soap making "snobbery" I'm sure you encountered while reading up on the processes.

MELT AND POUR PROCESS

Let's talk about the details of making melt-and-pour soap first before we talk about the others. The melt-and-pour process is exactly as the name says. You'll work with a meltable soap base – sometimes two, mix your color and scent and then pour the liquid into a mold and let it settle.

Once it cools down, you will need to take the finished soap out of the molds and you are done!. You can purchase these soap bases from the numerous soap-making sites you find online.

Three of the most popular brands are Castile, Brambleberry and bulk Apothecary. These are expressly made to be used in the melt-and-pour method. Don't confuse these soap bases with commercial soaps. This soap base is different from the soap you buy at your local beauty and bath shops.

After you melt and pour the soap, you can then add any colorings and scents as well as any other imaginative items. Some add small plastic flowers for decoration, others will add a small toy (be sure it won't melt) to entice children to take their baths and wash their hands before meals.

This method is perfect for those of us who don't aspire to be chemists and measure out the amount of lye for each batch they make. It's also the perfect activity to do with children. But even at this, the temperature of the melted soaps are a minimum of 150 degrees. So emphasize to your children, if they're helping you, that there are inherent dangers even in this process.

I prefer this method because I don't want to handle the potentially dangerous and harmful lye that you need with the hot process. If you don't feel you have an inner chemist -- and I definitely don't -- you may never be interested in the hot process.

Using the simple melt-and-pour method doesn't limit you in the wide variety of different soaps you can create. With a little time, you'll be making liquid, whipped, as well as bulk soap. And it goes without saying you can create fragrances by adding a variety of essential oils and decorating the soap to match anyone's personality or for any celebration. A baby or wedding shower, Christmas presents, birthday presents, etc.

People have added things like glitter and have embedded soap with clear soap. Before you know it, you will doing it too. Your only limitation in decorating or creating your soap is your own imagination. And, trust me, the more you "dabble" in your hobby, the more ideas you'll generate.

THE HOT PROCESS METHOD

This method actually begins by taking the lye and mixing it with water. Everyone who uses this process admits that this act alone can be dangerous. If you decide to give the hot process a try as you go along keep that in mind and work carefully.

Ironically, it matters exactly the order of the steps you mix these two ingredients. You must always add the lye to the water, never the other way around. If you pour the water into the lye you'll cause a minor "explosion."

If this should happen, it would be difficult to clean-up. That's guaranteed. But, what you actually need to worry about, is the danger involved in this minor "explosion."

Lye is often called a "caustic soda," aka sodium hydroxide. If it comes in contact with your skin, it's very likely to cause burns. This substance is also capable of corroding and eating through other substances.

You can see why until you're comfortable with the entire soap making process you may want to avoid using the hot-process method. And this is only the first step of the hot process method.

After that, the lye mixture is added to heated fat. Many people use their slow cooker for this step.

This blend is stirred for a while before you add anything more, like the dye for color or the fragrance ingredients or anything that will make it look more attractive.

Once you add all the ingredients, you'll still want to stir it for a bit longer. This ensures all the ingredients are evenly distributed. Once you're satisfied, they are you can then pour it into the mold of your choice.

THE COLD–PROCESS METHOD

That brings us to the cold process. Despite the name, this method is actually very similar to the hot process. The most notable difference is that in this method, the mixture is not heated during the stirring portion.

The fat is heated, but the lye, water, and fat mixture aren't. Some people refuse to use anything but soap made through this method. They swear that this technique creates soap that is, compared to any other, whether homemade or commercially processed, the most pampering on your skin.

They claim no other soap can even come close to softening the skin. After making soap for years now, I can respectfully disagree with this opinion, but hey, everyone is entitled to their own opinion right?

It's interesting to note that both the cold and hot processes rely on lye as the cornerstone of their methods. While you don't have to worry about handling lye with the melt-and-pour technique, you can be assured it's already in the soap base you're melting.

WHICH IS THE BEST PROCESS?

Without getting into this debate of which is a better process with anyone, let me just tell you-if the results are the same, why would you not pick the easiest process out of the three? Well, I did, and after trying the other two process, I was convinced that melt and pour is the best one of the bunch.

In fact, many professional soap makers advocate that beginners and children, as well as anyone who has a healthy fear and respect of the power and potential dangers of lye, would be better off using the melt-and-pour technique.

WHY LYE ANYWAY?

Lye, or as it's called in it chemical terms, sodium hydroxide, is a necessary part of every bar of soap. The reason you don't need to handle it when you're making soap with the melt-and-pour method is because this ingredient is already in the soap base you will be using.

This next fact about this chemical may surprise some of you, but you can't have soap if it doesn't contain lye. Any 'soap' without lye is merely detergent.

Lye, by the way, is a chemical made from ordinary salt. Once it's dissolved in water, in fact, it's not visible to the naked eye. Should you ever have the opportunity to work with it, you'll want to display extra special caution if you're working around children and pets.

Another aspect of lye that you need to keep in mind, is the amount of fumes it releases when it's mixed with water. For this reason, never stand directly over the mixture when you mix it, especially during the first thirty seconds.

The released fumes can trigger a choking sensation. The chemical mixture is blended with oil to eventually become soap which is a process call saponify. Soaps vary a great deal in terms of their ingredients.

For example, while some soaps make your skin dry, other soaps are very moisturizing. Glycerin soaps are considered to be one of the most moisturizing types of soap.

The unique quality of this type of soap allows it to be both moisturizing and effective for all different kinds of skin. The benefits of glycerin soap help your skin become healthy and moisturize.

CHAPTER 3: ALL THE SUPPLIES AND EQUIPMENT YOU'LL EVER NEED

TOOLS AND EQUIPMENT

The double-boiler is about to become your best friend as you discover how easy it is to work with. It is essentially a two pot solution for safely melting your soap base with burning it up. You'll need the double boiler in order to melt the wax without keeping your soap on the stove too long and burning it.

Some prefer to melt their soap in a microwave oven. Here again, you run the risk of burning it or melting it too fast.

If you have a double boiler already that you cook with, you can simply use that. But you'll have to be careful when washing it. There's nothing worse than taking a bite out of your soup and instead you're tasting soap. It won't make you sick, it isn't harmful. It's just not extremely tasty.

Of course, if you don't have a double boiler you can always get by nicely by placing a metal bowl over a saucepan with water. You'll get the same effect. It is, however, easier to use the double boiler. Expect to pay around $20-$50 for one of these based on their size.

You'll also want to consider buying stainless steel pots. It won't matter at this moment with melt and pour, but you'll be glad you have these should you start working with lye. Lye tends to corrode other pans over a relatively short time period.

AN INSTANT READ THERMOMETER

It is vital to have an instant-read thermometer to measure the temperature of the soap the moment it's been poured or right before you pour it into the mold. In these cases, you simply can't wait even the few moments some thermometers take to register the temperature.

If you have a local craft store in your area, you can simply get one there. Or better yet, why not purchase two if you don't already have one in your kitchen? In this way, should you ever need to check the temperature of two containers simultaneously, you'll have no trouble doing it. Expect to pay around $7-$20 for one of this.

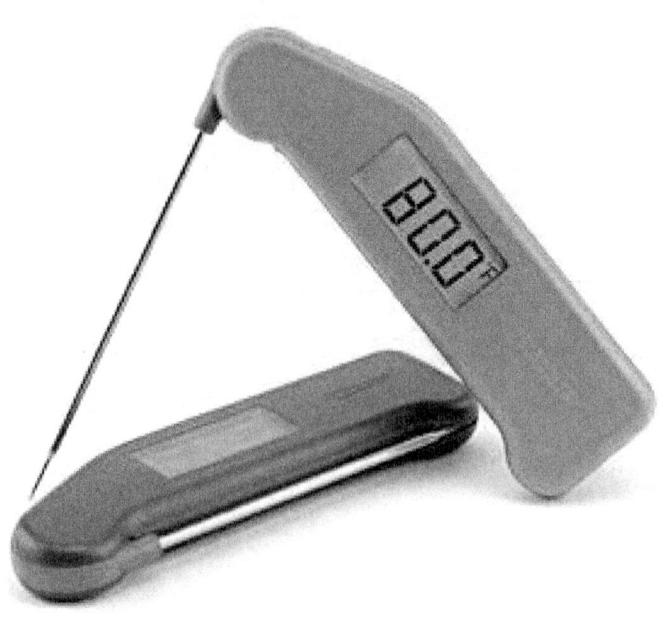

A SCALE

You'll need a scale because the recipes from which you're working will require you to weigh out specific amounts of soap, usually indicated in ounces. When you're working with the pour-and-melt technique, you won't need a scale quite as accurate as with the cold or hot process.

But if you don't already have a scale and can afford it, think about getting one that is also suitable for making soap with lye. Many people love soap-making so much that they "move up" to the hot or cold process or both. A typical scale like the one on the picture should not cost you more than $35.

RUBBING ALCOHOL

You'll want to be sure that you have rubbing alcohol in a spray bottle handy. If you should see bubbles forming on the soap after you pour it, you'll be surprised at how a quick spritz or two eliminates them nearly magically.

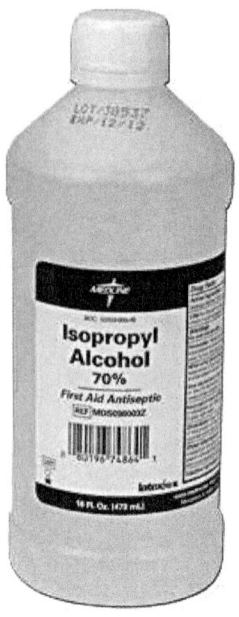

Alcohol also helps you to prepare the surface of soap that's already been cooled. It'll help embeddable objects adhere while you're working on the second round of pouring. You can pick one of these bottles at any grocery store for around $1.50

SPRAY BOTTLE

Buy some medium size plastic spray bottles that you can find in any stores like Walmart, Target or any other stores.

CUTTING BOARD

You need a non-slip cutting board to cut and shape your soaps, I prefer to use a white non wood cutting board, but pick the one you are comfortable working with. Typical cost for one of these boards are around $12-$15

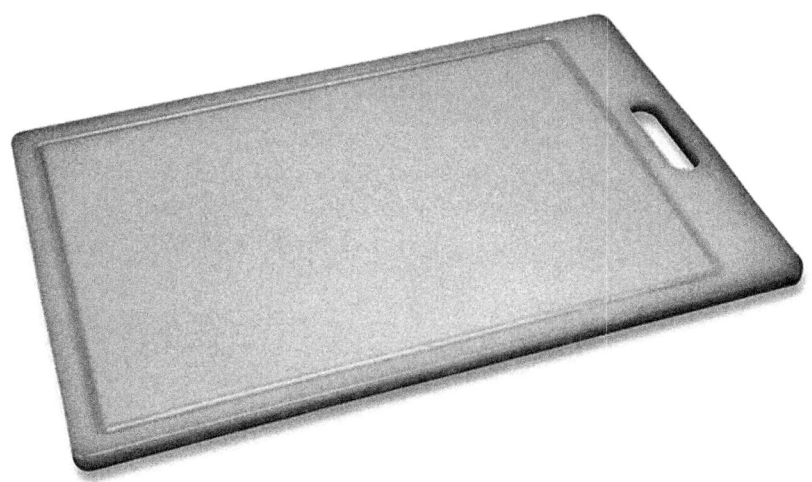

You will need a knife/cutter to cut your soaps into shape. Buy a quality knife that is sharp and not to thin or light, as you will need something moderately heavy duty one for this task. Expect to pay around $15 for one.

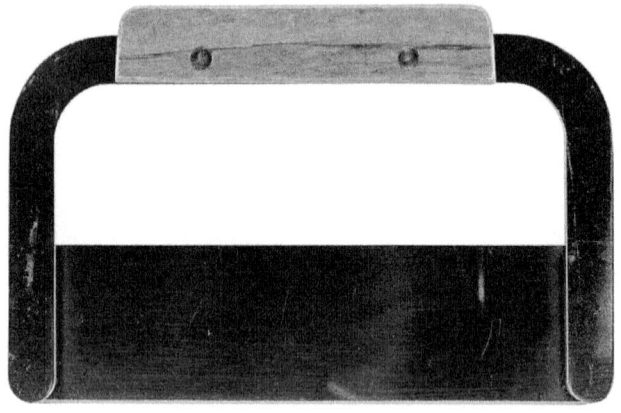

SOAP MAKING MATERIAL

THE SOAP BASE

The two most common brands of melt-and-pour soap bases are Castile and Brambleberry. Each of these suppliers have their own presence on the web, as well as purchasing them through any number of soap-making sites and even (surprise!) amazon.com.

(Brambleberry Base)

If you're not sure about these brands, you can discover what others use simply by visiting craft shows and asking those behind the homemade soap tables. Just tell them you're learning the craft and you would like their opinion as well as what type they use. Don't worry. On the whole, these people will be delighted to answer any of your questions.

Many people tell me they buy their soap base from eBay. I've never bought mine this way, but you can give it a try. I just feel more comfortable buying supplies from digital or brick-and-mortar stores.

One word of caution is to be sure to buy melt-and-pour soap base, "ordinary" soap base will not work. It doesn't melt. How do I know this? You guessed it, I bought the wrong type and regardless what I did, the soap refused to melt.

As for cost, depending on which supplier you buy from, a typical good quality base will cost you around $7.50 - $15 per pound, but always look for bulk deals, this is when you get them in 25 lb. bags with a huge discount.

Of course, you'll want to add color to your soap! Even on your first encounter with this hobby. You'll be delighted to know that not only are plenty of colors from which you can choose, but there are plenty of different ways to do it.

You can use mica (which we talk about a little later) liquid colorants, like those from Lab Colors natural colorants and so much more.

If you buy your soap from an online soap-making business, take the time to look around the site, some of these sites provide you with marvelous alternatives – far too many to even begin to describe here.

Most surprising of all is how affordable these products are. And they'll make your soap look like a million bucks.

(Color Block)

One of my friends loves coloring her soaps with Color Blocks. These are nothing more than small pieces of melt-and-pour soap, highly concentrated and already mixed with various oxides, micas, and pigments. They're simple to use. All you do is to add a small amount of the color block to your batch of melted soap and stir.

This is a great technique to use because it prevents clumping and speckles. And of course, it's so easy to just use as part of your soap bases. This is an especially good method to use for on your first couple projects. Children love working with these as well.

The heat takes care of all the difficult work. It melts the shavings which then colors the soap. Simply add Color Block to melted soap and stir. The heat melts the Color Block shavings, which color the soap. Color Blocks are great for preventing clumps and speckles, and incorporate easily into the melt-and-pour bases.

Here is the Brambleberry site for all melt and pour color blocks, take a look. https://www.brambleberry.com/Color-Blocks-for-Melt-Pour--C340.aspx

SCENT AND FRAGRANCE

What is soap without a refreshing scent and fragrance? So even on your first attempt, you should try your hand adding some scent in your soap. It's as easy as buying simple essential oils and adding a drop or two to your soap while it's melted.

When I say "essential oils" I mean the type you probably already have at home, the type you put in your diffuser. If you don't happen to have any, you can buy them at just about any health food store, sometimes in pharmacies, and of course, always online.

MOLDS

Another critical category of supplies you'll need is the soap mold. Well, at least some type of mold.

You can use the same molds that you use for your candy-making. Many people, though, prefer to start this new hobby with new molds dedicated to your soap-making hobby.

As you look through the recipes presented here and on the web, you'll discover one of the most popular and most useful is what's called a "block mold." It really is a large block. Once you use it you'll understand the name. It's merely a large block, and you'll pour a large amount of soap into it. Once the soap in the mold gels and hardens, then from here you'll cut it into smaller bars.

Later in the book, once we get you crafting, we'll talk about the various molds available to you. If you can't wait to check them out, you may want to review Chapter 5 quickly, just to satisfy your curiosity.

CHAPTER 4: INSTRUCTIONS FOR A BASIC MELT-AND-POUR PROJECT

Because melt-and-pour soap is such an easy process, you can easily place additional items into your soap even on your first venture. In the initial project I've included several additives, including "fragrance" and color. After all what good is soap if doesn't have a pleasing scent to it and a bit of color?

INGREDIENTS

Melt-and-pour soap base: either clear or opaque or both

Soap coloring

Cosmetic grade scent or essential oils

Rubbing alcohol

EQUIPMENT

Microwave or Double Boiler

-If you use a microwave for melting the soap, then you want several **microwaveable plastic or glass**

containers or jars with pouring spouts to make the pouring easier.

-**A dowel rod or other instrument** with which to stir the soap occasionally

-**Glass container (for the melted soap)**

-**Small spray bottle for rubbing alcohol**

-**Mold of your choice**

-**Clear plastic wrap**

You'll want to wrap the soap as soon as possible because it shouldn't be exposed to the air for very long.

-**A chopping/cutting board**

-**Knife or grater**

Cutting the soap in inch cubes or grating it will help the soap melt faster.

-**A scale**

-Small eye droppers if you're using powdered colorant

DIRECTIONS

Place your empty glass container on the scale. Zero the weight out.

Make sure that all of the equipment that will be touching the soap is clean.

Cut your soap into small chunks – about one-inch squares – until you have the amount that fits into your mold.

Don't worry if you're not exactly right. A couple tenth of an ounce either over or under is not going affect the filling of the mold.

Cover the glass container with cling wrap, to prevent the soap base from drying out as you're heating it. Place this in the microwave and begin heating it. Start slowly. Initially, you'll only want to keep it in the microwave for a minute at a time, maximum.

Remove the container from the microwave and stir the soap. At this point, after only a minute of heat, the soap should be thick and chunky. Place the container back into the microwave for another minute, then take it out and stir again. Do this several more times, for no longer than a minute at a time. After several minutes, you may even want to shorten the heating periods to 45 or 30 seconds. In this way, you can keep a close eye on it.

By the time the soap melts it should be at about 150 degrees, so handle this carefully. You'll know when the soap is melted because the chunks will have disappeared.

While the soap is heating, you can take whatever small container you're going to place the fragrance or essential oil in on the scale and zero out the weight. Measure your fragrance or essential oil of your choice into this container. For a pound of soap, approximately 0.4 ounces of the oil is an excellent starting point. Feel free to adjust the oil to suit your liking by putting a bit more in so the next time you make soap it will a bit less.

Once you've prepared the amount of essential oil and it's already in its own container, you can remove the soap from the microwave and slowly add the fragrance to the melted base. Stir the oil into the soap slowly and gently.

The next step is to add a bit of color to your soap. Just be sure that the colors you add are soap and skin safe, micas or natural colorants.

Stir the melted soap thoroughly to ensure both the fragrance and the color blend fully into the soap. While you want to blend them well, **don't** stir them quickly or you'll have bubbles in the soap.

Should you discover bubbles, don't worry about it. This is where you'll recall, the rubbing alcohol comes in handy. Simply spray a bit of the alcohol on them. The bubbles should disappear.

TA! DA!

Now you can start cleaning up.

It should only take a few hours for the soap to harden. If you're impatient, or need it sooner, you can hasten this process by placing the mold in the refrigerator, but don't put it into the freezer. If soap is hardening in the refrigerator, it should only take about an hour.

Recognizing that people have different methods of learning, I've included below a YouTube video of an individual making a simple melt-and-pour batch of soap. It's not the same recipe I've just given you, but it is an excellent one to watch.

If you recall, I first had to go watch my friend make soap before I became convinced I could do it on my own. If you watch this, I hope it convinces you to give this amazing hobby a try.

https://www.youtube.com/watch?v=eE3PPlY3_8E

START A JOURNAL

You'll probably be excited by the first couple of batches of soap you make, you'll be standing over the soap watching it hardened. Instead of doing that, why not take a notebook during this time, sit down with a cup of coffee or tea and write your experience in a notebook. Among the things you'll want to include is the number of drops of color you used as well as how much fragrance.

In this way when you review the bar, you'll know how to adjust these items for the next soap-making session. If you think you've placed too much scent in the bar, then you'll know exactly what you placed in there. And this will give you an idea of how much you may want to cut back on that ingredient. This record keeping is vital for your first several projects, because you may not remember.

Later, as you use this recipe more often, the amount of scent or color will become second nature. But you'd be wise not to try to test your memory at the very beginning. Be sure to record if you have any soap left over after you've poured the soap into the mold.
Once the soap has hardened completely, you'll be able to easily remove the bars out of the mold.

Depending on the type of mold you've used, you may have bit of a challenge. Not to worry. If the soap doesn't come out on its own, simply tap the back of the mold with the palm of your hand or even a large spoon to see if you can't encourage them to pop out.

If after all, the bar is still stubbornly refusing to pop out, then turn the mold over and run hot water over it. You'll discover the soap will fall out for you.

Your next step is to give your soap a good inspection. If you discover any imperfections, simply trim or rub them off. You can use a cloth or if they're stubborn do this with a small knife. Just be careful if you choose the latter.

Now, here's the best part. Your soap is already cured. So you don't need to wait impatiently for a curing process to occur.

Go ahead. Take a bar and use one right away if you'd like.

CHAPTER 5: SOAP MOLDS AND MORE SOAP MOLDS

WHERE DO I BEGIN?

There are so many types of molds you can use. Most of them are easy to use, and all of them produce beautiful bars of soap. Now, more than ever thanks to the internet, you now have so many types of molds to pick from for the melt-and-pour soap.

No longer are you limited in choice by what you have in your local craft supply store or even the limited direct-mail catalogs that everyone used to receive.

Block molds are also essential when you make soap of different colors.

(Block Soap Molds)

WHY USE A MOLD AT ALL?

You could do without block molds or any type of dedicated mold at all. Use anything you have at home that could hold hot, liquid soap. This is especially exciting if you're flexible in the shape of the final hardened "bar" of soap. The truth is, if you use your imagination, you can use nearly anything in its place. Consider using just a standard serving-ware container.

In fact, in some ways, the end product will turn out even better than you may think. As the soap sets, it'll mold around any of the bumps, mold marks, and curves of the containers. These can add interest to the product as well as welcome detail that makes it an individual bar.

If you don't care for that or find it attractive you can simply scrape these areas away using a paring knife, cheese plane or even a dough scraper.

LONG NARROW MOLDS

You may want to invest in a couple long narrow molds in case you want to make what's referred to as "loaves."

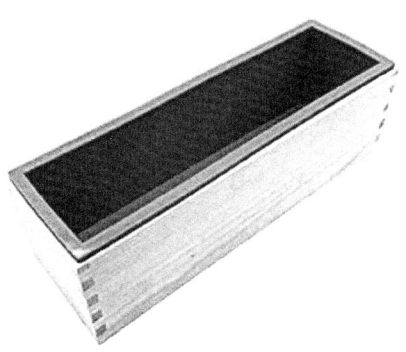

(Long Narrow Mold)

These come in both oblong shapes, where the length of the mold is greater than the height as well as square. In either case, you'll pour the melted soap in here along with the scents and colorants.

You can find these molds in different sizes, but one of the most common sizes is the square mold which is approximately 9 ¼ inches long, 2 ¾ inches deep and at its widest point 3 ¼ inches.

While these molds are most commonly associated with the melt-and-pour soap-making process, they're also appropriate to use for the cold-process technique as well.

You'll discover some loaf molds can't take temperatures ranging up to 135 or 145 degrees Fahrenheit. If you have any doubts about the temperature of your melted soap, test the temperature before pouring it. If the temperature gets too high, it can warp the plastic mold.

The soap will be the easiest to release from this type of mold 12 to 14 hours after cooling. Don't force the soap to release. If you're having problem getting the hardened soap out, put them in the freezer for about 30 minutes.

You really needn't be overly concerned about washing these containers. They are easiest to clean after you soak them in warm water for about 30 minutes. **Do not – I repeat – do not** place them in your dishwasher, as tempting as that may be. They indeed can be subject to warping in hot water of the appliance.

Oh, and by the way, these loaf molds cost in the range of $12.95 to 14.95, perhaps a bit more in some locations. But, considering that you can make anywhere from half a dozen to even a dozen of bars of soap in one sitting, the price is reasonable. Of course, only you can decide if this fits your budget.

BAR MOLDS

These come in a variety of forms themselves. You can find them as plain or as intricate as you'd like. The fanciest, most elegant bar molds can be found with beautifully detailed designs, befitting even the most elegant bathroom.

(Bar Mold)

The bar mold is sometimes considered the staple of soap-making mold and these days they're even easier than ever to work with, thanks to the flexible, silicone versions. Like the plastic loaf molds we spoke of earlier, these work well with the melt-and-pour method as well as the cold-process method.

That's good to know if you ever decide one day to test drive making soap using the cold-process technique.

This mold is the perfect one when you're making soap and the bars need to be uniform in size. They also come in handy when you're testing fragrances and colors. The cavities in these molds are rectangular, but they have no taper, which means you don't need to be concerned with cutting in a straight line. That, by the way, is not a talent I was born with.

The amazing aspect of these silicone molds is the amount of heat it can withstand – up to 440 degrees Fahrenheit. If you plan to move this type of mold *after* you've poured the soap and before it's set, then make sure you set it on a tray or a cookie sheet **before** you actually pour it.

Silicone, after all, is flexible and you may end up with a shape or two you hadn't expected if you don't take this precaution.

Under normal circumstances, you don't need to worry about what happens when you go to loosen the soap from the mold. The soap should come off easily, effortlessly and without any damage from the mold.

The only disadvantage of working with silicone molds is that they take a little more care when you clean them. Of course, you start by washing them well. Then you spritz them with a bit of that rubbing alcohol. (See how handy this little spray jar is becoming!) The alcohol will lift out any lingering scents. Then, you'll want to wash it again.

You may want to try working with one of these. Your best bet is to use a bar mold that makes 12 bars each one holding a four-ounce bar. The typical bar mold is about 2 by 3 inches and 1 ½ inches deep.

Look around. Possible molds are everywhere, practically crying to be chosen as part of your projects.

It's true. And once you delve into this hobby, you will be surprised at discovering possible molds in your home, especially in your kitchen. Think ice cube trays and plastic gelatin molds for starters. And don't forget to take a quick look in your recycling bin. Yes. As you look, think about how cool the little bumps on the bottom of plastic soda bottles could be very cool when embedded into a bar of soap.

All you need to do is to cut the planned molded shape from the rest of the bottle itself using a heavy pair of scissors. For safety's sake, it's best to wear some type of protective glasses or goggles. You'll also want to be careful not to cut your hands on the sharp parts of the bottle, once they're cut.

How often you're planning on using your molds will be a deciding factor in the strength and thickness of the mold that's best for you. If you're not planning to use molds frequently, then a lighter weight mold, made of thinner plastic is fine. But if you believe that you'll be using them quite a bit, then you may want the heavier type. These will last longer for you.

Whatever type you buy, though, you'll want to handle them carefully when you wash and dry them. Wash them in warm water and dish detergent, ensuring they're completely clean.

Dry them flat, so they don't warp.

Obviously, the heavier gauge plastic your mold is made of, the longer they will serve you well. That doesn't mean you can abuse them. They still need to be handled gently and with care just as you'll discover all the other molds do.

Eventually, any mold, regardless of the type of plastic it's made of, will crack given enough use even when you handle it properly.

TRAY MOLDS AND MORE

At some point, you may decide that you'll want to use a tray mold. This is a mold with a single cavity that contains score marks. You use these marks as guides when you cut your soap into bars after you take them out of the mold.

You can purchase these molds "bare bones," that is with no decorations. You can also find them with wonderfully delightful designs. I have some with lavender stems on them and others with drawings of animal figures. I like to think of these as a "hybrid" of block and bar molds.

(Tray mold)

When it comes to purchasing three-dimensional molds, you've got such a large variety from which to choose, you'll have trouble deciding.

You can use, what are called, "two-part molds" that you fasten together, seal them and then pour your soap into them. Once the soap has hardened, then you take the clips off and simply release the form.

On these, you'll need to remove the mold lines, the points at which the two sides of the molds came together. This will give your soap a finished, professional look.

Soap on a rope never seems to go out of style, probably because it's so convenient to store. You can find the ropes either at your local soap-crafting store or online. It's easy enough to create. You simply embed the rope into the three-dimensional bar

While you're shopping for molds, you don't want to overlook the vinyl molds. To release the hardened soap from these, you simply pull the soap away from the top and sides. It's that simple.

Then there are the silicone molds. You release the soap from these by stretching the silicon and peeling the hardened soap off.

No discussion of soap molds is complete with talking about tube molds. These are among the most exciting ways to add gorgeous detail to your projects by embedding a variety of shapes from this mold.
Tube molds are literally long tubes, and you can find them in a variety of shapes. You pour the warm soap into the tube making sure it's full.

Allow the soap inside it to harden and then push it out. Yep, it's that simple. Now you have a long piece of soap that you can use to embed in another project either whole or you can cut them into pieces.

WHEN ALL ELSE FAILS, IMPROVISE

I'm serious. You can buy a small piece of pipe in order to make thin rods of soap. You can use a bit larger piece of pipe to make bigger rods. These are also perfect if you're thinking about casting round bars of soap.

Simply punch out the soap when it hardens cut them into smaller bars. If you find you're struggling to remove the soap from the pipe, simply freeze them before popping them out.

One of the easiest way to make a pipe and probably one of the least expensive is to buy PVC pipe at your local hardware store. You can get it cut to your specifications. You can also buy caps to fit the ends of the pipe. In this way, you don't have to be concerned about how to seal the mold. Think about buying screw on, threaded caps for ease of removal.

You can, however, buy stainless steel tubes in various geometric shapes or animal shapes. These are most easily located in cake decorating and gourmet stores. They were made to be bread molds, believe it or not, for canapes, but they are perfect for soap making as well. You may decide you want to embed stars into your next soap project. It's easy enough with a tube of this shape.

VERTICAL MOLDS

No, we're not quite done talking about molds. There's a newer type of mold that you may want to take a look at. You'll hear it referred to either as a tube mold or as a vertical mold. Some of these molds come in distinct pieces which you clamp together when you're ready to fill them. And, of course, unclamp them and pull the two halves apart when the soap inside has hardened.

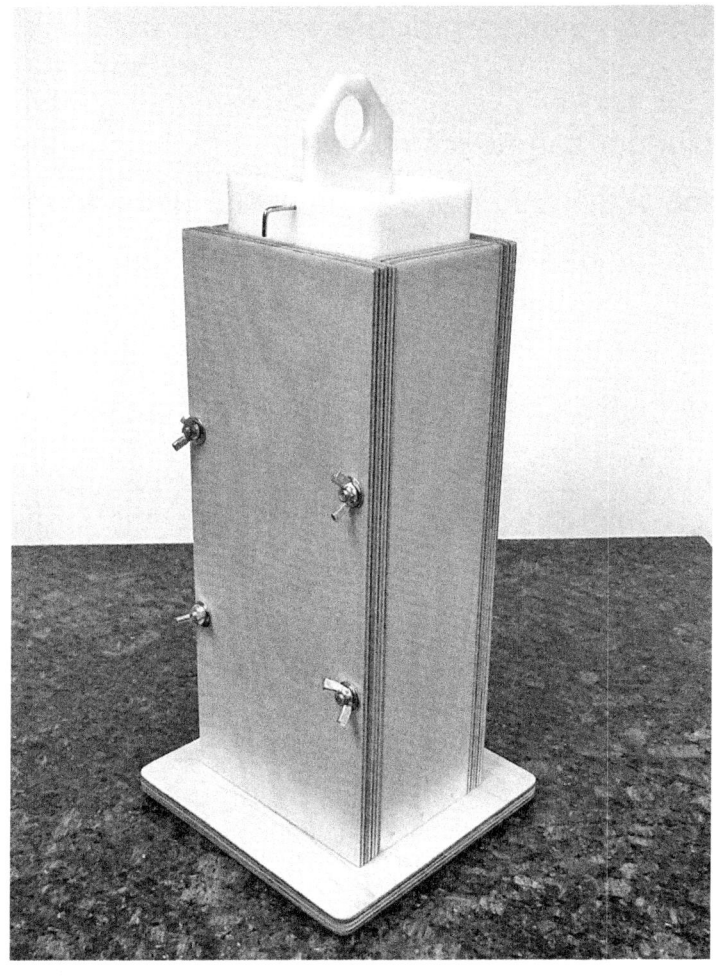

(Vertical Mold)

I'm not going to lie to you, you'll come across times that you discover you're just plain frustrated. You'll run into difficulty in getting the soap out of a mold. In order to avoid that frustration (remember first and foremost this is supposed to be a fun hobby!) create your own plungers for these moments.

A plunger can be something as simple as a disk of wood which you place in the tube. Using a stick, you push the disk so it can dislodge the soap from the pipe.

LEARNING THE TYPES OF SOAP CASTING PROJECTS

If you're not familiar with soap making, you may think that there isn't much difference in implementing different styles of projects. You melt and pour, and you've done.

And for the single pour projects, it's almost that easy. But it gets a bit more involved when you move from single pour to embedded objects and even block over pours.

Once you learn the basics, you'll be more than ready to try all the kinds of casting projects this type of soap making is capable of.

It's best to start with the basic and then move to the more involved projects. The simplest, as you might guess is the single pour into block molds. This is the most basic of the techniques, you once you learn this, you can graduate to more intricate exercises.

Before you even begin this project, give some thought to the type of block mold you would like to use. Of course, you can buy one at the many outlets that advertise on the internet as well as on eBay or Etsy. You can also go to your local craft store to buy one.

But there is a third object for block molds. And it's as close as your kitchen For a single pour casting project like the one you're about to do, you can rummage through your kitchen cabinets and find a suitable substitute.

First look through all of your plastic storage containers. You'll need to find one that is not only heat resistant and flexible but also be the dimensions that you'll find it relatively easy to divide the bars into your desired size.

Longer, deeper containers are perfect for "loaf" molds. Square, shallow containers are great to use for bars that are squared shape. Once the soap in this container has hardened, you can cut the soap into bars much like you do brownies. But you don't have to stop there.

Think about pouring soap that can be used as smaller pieces that you'll eventually use in another as well. For example, strips of soaps or chunks can look quite pleasing as embedded objects used in another soap-casting technique.

How can you tell the container or even the mold you plan on using will hold the amount of soap you'd like to melt? If you need to check the volume, fill the container or mold with water. Then pour that into a measuring cup to determine how much liquid soap you'll require.

You can either adjust your recipe accordingly to the container you've chosen or just keep looking until you find a closer fit.

CHAPTER 6: ADDING COLOR TO YOUR SOAP

Adding color and creating colorful soap is without a doubt my favorite part of the soap-making process. It's true. When you create soap using this method, you have the freedom to use color made of just about any types of ingredients. The only limits you have is your own imagination.

That's because this soap base not only accepts just about all types of pigments but makes it looks fabulous at the same time. One of the most exciting aspects of this is that you can even mix colors made with different ingredients.

COLOR THEORY

Before we even get into the various forms of color that are available to you when you use the melt-and-pour method, I would be remiss if I didn't spend at least a bit of time talking about something that sounds boring: "color theory."

In fact, it isn't boring at all but a necessary component of your basic soap-making education. Unless you're trained as a graphic designer or an artist, the art of combining colors probably isn't in your wheelhouse. Of course, we all have an eye when it comes to colors we love together.

But when you learn even a small amount about color theory, you won't have to worry that those who receive your gifts will appreciate your color combinations.

Color theory certainly wasn't in my wheelhouse when I first began this adventure. And, it's the first thing many novice soap makers ask me about: mixing colors without disastrous effects.

Let's face it. You're adding color to your soap to enhance its attractiveness.

Color theory, for the most, talks about color in light and in pigment. You'll find that those who work with colors on computer screens or theatrical lighting are most concerned with the effects of color in the light.

On the other hand, those who paint on canvasses, fabrics and other crafts would be more concerned with the effects of color in pigment. Glasswork, for example, is the one craft that comes to mind that works with the effects of color both in the light as well as pigment.

Bear with the elementary science lesson for a few moments. You'll discover that this short lesson will immensely help your understanding of color and save time and – at least at the start – misery and disaster.

The colors on pigmented surfaces are actually a transmission of the spectrum. What your eyes see and report back to the brain as color, are in reality, light waves. These waves are transmitted to your retina in the back of your eyes. If you have a difficult time grasping the abstract idea of a spectrum of light, substitute the word rainbow.

That's exactly what a spectrum of light is. It just doesn't sound as scientific. But it's a much better way to visualize it.

And we all know the colors as ROY G. BIV: red, orange, yellow, green, blue, indigo and violet. When white light is directed at a painting on a canvass, you see those colors on the surface. If, however, you're viewing that same surface, same colors with a tinted light, the color that's transmitted to your brain will be altered. How it's changed will depend on the color of the light and the color of the pigment.

Most of the time, you'll be viewing your soap under "normal" conditions or white light, so this won't be much of an issue. The only time it was for me, when my daughter, who was a teenager at the time, took a bar of blue soap and turned on her orange light. Then it looked black, and for a few moments, she thought of her mother as a genius.

THE COLOR WHEEL

A color wheel is probably one of the most useful tools in your toolkit when you're considering choices for your soaps. A graphic artist showed me his color wheel, and from that moment on, I knew that I had to have one of my own to save me time and aggravation.

We all learned the mixture of colors in school – whether it was elementary school or in art class in high school. But it's not something we think about as an adult – unless you decide to make soap.

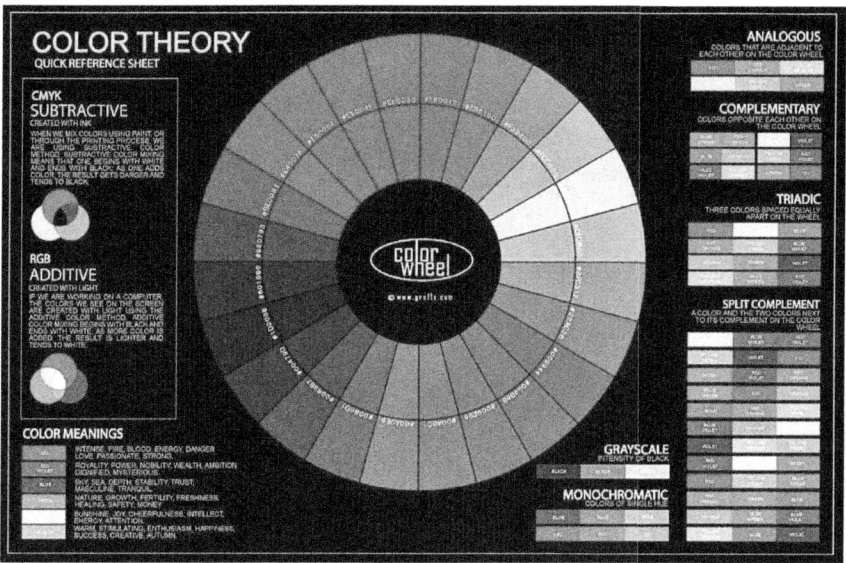

You can purchase one inexpensively online or at your local art supply store. Many soap makers have created their own color wheel, but unless you fundamentally understand how one works, it's difficult to do. Not only that, right now, your mind is focused on soap making.

Later on, you may decide to make one or better yet, help your children make their own so they can help understand colors and – here's the real reason – stop grabbing yours and playing with it. But that's a project best kept for a rainy or snow-bound day when your children are clamoring for something to do.

Once you have your color wheel in hand, you want to check out what are called the complementary colors. They can be found because believe it or not, they'll be on opposite sides of the wheel. Start with checking out the primary colors.

A primary color is one in which is the most basic in composition. Primary colors are blue, yellow, and red. They can't be created by adding two colors together. These are in fact, three colors that are combined to get all the other colors on the wheel.

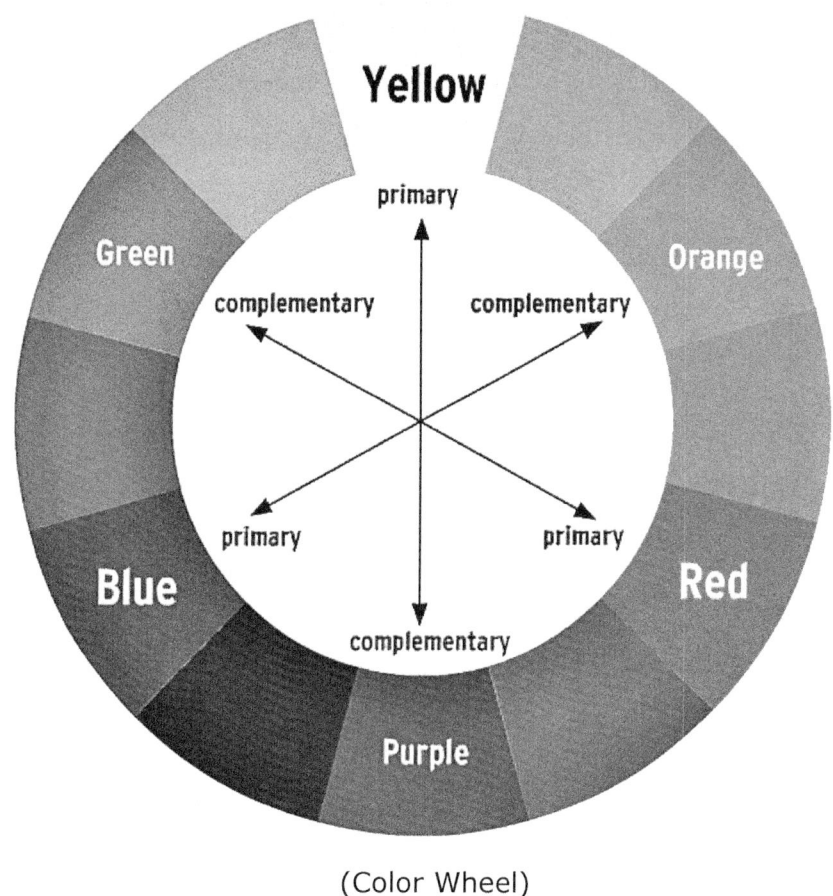

(Color Wheel)

Any color that isn't yellow, blue or red is secondary or even tertiary colors. That is they're colors created by combining the primary ones in some form.

Observe what color is opposite the primary color yellow on the color wheel. It's the secondary color purple. The color across from the primary color of red is green and directly across from primary blue is secondary orange. You'll find some wonderful color combinations hidden in here.

COLOR STORIES

It's a unique name for a phenomenon we all take for granted. Answer this question: What colors do you think of when someone talks about the season autumn? Probably shades of browns and oranges and hues of earth tones.

And what about spring colors? What colors do you inherently use to welcome spring into your home? I'm sure you immediately thought of pastels, glorious light pastels.

Each of those is a color story. What color story might you use if the mom-to-be had no preference in making her soap? Of course blue and pink.
Fashion designers do this when they advertise "new fall colors."

Now, you're about to write your own color story. Don't worry, you don't have to be a word wizard in order to carry this off. Walk into your bathroom and create a color story based on that room. Examine the colors you already have in there. List the colors of the paint or wallpaper, the tiles, the fixtures and even the decorative accents.

This is the foundation for your bathroom's color story.

I'm going to use a fictional bathroom to walk you through your first color story. The paint in the room is a pale pink. The tile is white with a thin, pale blue-green accent border. The towels are a light sage green.

Now, with your color wheel in hand, you're going to unravel the components of this color story. When you see these colors on the wheel, the first thing you'll probably notice is that the pale pink and the light sage green are actually complementary colors, albeit in a lighter version of red and green.

You'll also observe that blue-green is sitting next to green on the wheel on the blue side. There you have it.

You have a complementary pastel motif with a tertiary accent.

MICA

Love glittering soap? Then you'll want to add mica to your soap base. Mica is the name of a group of natural minerals of the earth. They're mined, purified then ground finely into powder. These are used for a myriad of applications.

Soap making and cosmetics are just one category. It gets its natural pearlescent sparkle and metallic appearance thanks to its fragile, layered crystalline structure. Mica, by the way, is the ingredient in metallic paint that gives cars their attractive glitter.

The mica used in soap-making often is a more complex ingredient than just the powdered mineral. Many times these simple powders are enhanced with iron oxide or titanium dioxide coating, giving the coloring a multi-layered complex appearance.

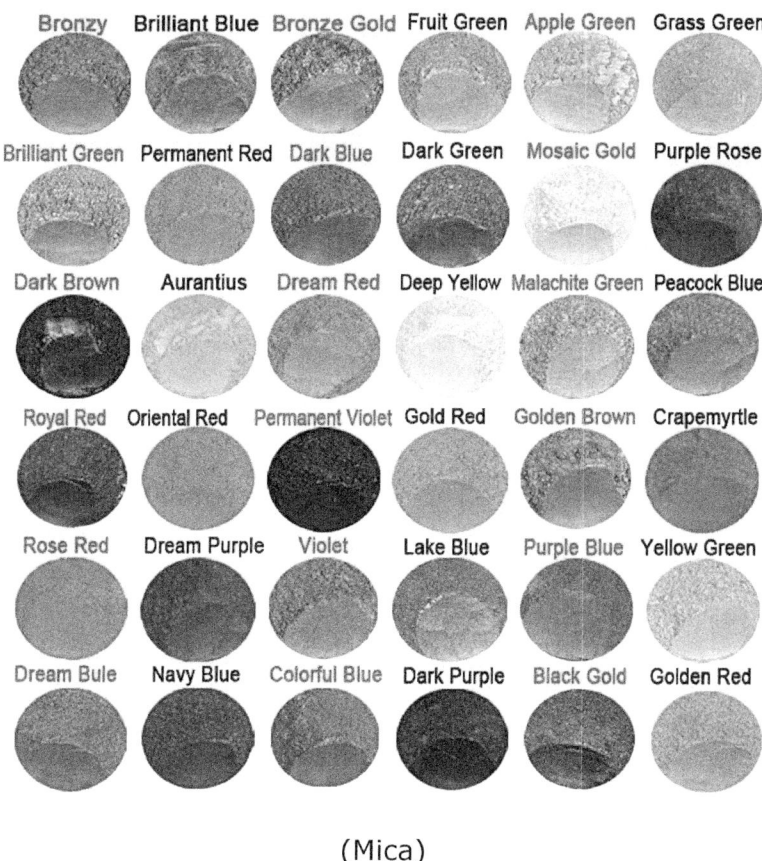

(Mica)

Mica's attractiveness relies on light reflected off the soap. This is why you'll see it at its peak colors in transparent soaps – especially the melt and pour.

Yes! You can get this effect in the soap you make. And it takes very little effort.

Start with approximately a half of teaspoon of mica for every pound of soap you use. This is the basis for the pearlescent effect.

But don't stop there. Include other colors in the soap along with the mica. You may want to add just a small smattering of the mineral – don't stir it throughout the entire bar. Instead just swirl a bit in. You'll be amazed at how this looks once it hardens.

Some soap makers actually brush the mica into the mold, giving the final product a type of jeweled effect. This particular technique may take a while to master. You'll need to get the melted soap at the right temperature. If it's too hot when you pour, the mica will just be washed to the bottom of the mold.

You'll be able to tell if it's too hot by the viscosity of the soap. If it's too thin, then your soap is too hot for the procedure. If this is the case, though, just continue to stir the mixture until it does thicken.

COLOR MY WORLD – WITH PIGMENTS

When you decide you're ready to try your hand at some serious colorings in your soap, you'll want to look at something called pigments. These are easy enough to use when you're only using a single color in your soap. There will come a time, though, when you'll want to use several colors in a bar. Who wouldn't?

Soaps with several colors look so stunning, you may, at first glance, seem like it's difficult to do. You may simply dismiss that you can mix pigments yourself, with results just as stunning as those you're admiring now.

For this effect, you'll need to use pigment powder. You'll want to start at $1/8^{th}$ of a teaspoon of the powder for every pound of melted soap base. You don't want to use too much because that can cause the pigment to run and stain surfaces.

While the name of this soap-making process is melt-and-pour, it really is a bit more than that. Once you start getting proficient at it and you use different colors and add other items into your soap, you'll learn probably its two most important aspects. The fact is that timing and temperatures are important. The same goes for adding pigment.

Once you've completed melting your soap base and you've decided and completed the mixture of your pigments, you'll drop it into the soap base. But, the best time to do this is when the base is about 120 degrees Fahrenheit. When you add it at this temperature, it increases the viscosity and prevents the pigments from running.

If you only add about half of the recommended mixture, you'll end up with pastel colors. Adding the entire mixture, as you might guess, provides with a deeper, richer darker shades.

The other aspect of coloring you should keep in mind when you use colors is that the same color can look different under different lighting conditions and according to who's viewing it. As you use more pigments, you'll discover you're being flexible in your use of them. This is especially true if you're not using a recipe, but experimenting for the best results.

Also if you're thinking of improvising, don't forget you can use food coloring to the melted base. If you do this, start with one drop of color and then add one drop more at a time until you get your desired color.

You'll soon discover that coloring your soap is one of the most satisfying aspects of your new soap-making hobby.

But wait, there's more! What's soap with colors, if there are no scents in your soap to draw in all of your five senses, to draw you into that bathtub for the luxurious, relaxing bath?

In the next chapter, we'll learn what scents and fragrances to use depending on who is going to use your soap and what effect they want from it.

CHAPTER 7: ADDING ESSENTIAL OILS AS SCENT

Essential oils are more popular than ever before. Not only do they carry singular incredible scents, but they also soothe your nerves, boost your energy level, and in some cases people say these oils can help in healing various ailments of your body and soul.

There's even an entire branch of study that's dedicated to understanding what scents help both your body to heal and your mind relax, destress and even may help improve your productivity. It's referred to as aromatherapy.

However you feel about certain scents, the fragrance of a soap influences your thoughts more than you even realize.

Now that you're making soap, the decision of the fragrance and scent of the bars are in your hands. If you're not familiar with essential oils and how they affect our bodies, here is a short list of the most common ones used in soap making. This list is by no means inclusive. But it will give you some guidelines to get you started using these oils. In no time at all, you'll be an expert on essential oils, aromatherapy, and how you can use them most effectively in your hobby.

LAVENDER

This is probably the most loved all the essential oils – and with good reason. It's probably the most versatile of all the oils, if you have any type of health challenge. Its legendary healing reputation begins with your nervous system; it's a pain-killer, it disinfects your scalp and skin and enhances blood circulation. Additionally, it has been known to help respiratory health challenges.

If you one of your teenage children is suffering from acne, you may want to make her or him a bar with this essential oil in it. Lavender has long been known as a natural remedy for oily skin and acne.

ROSEMARY

There are many varieties of this herb each with its own signature aroma and individual healing potential. You'll find one with a more camphor-like smell, which may make it just the ticket for someone who finds themselves in need of healing from colds and flu, especially if they've settled in your chest.

There's another, popular scent that is woody and makes a great masculine fragrance for soap for men. Rosemary makes a wonderful unique scent when mixed any number of other scents. Think of mixing it with aromas like orange, peppermint, cedar wood, and even with lavender. Just let your imagination go and trust your intuition.

LEMON

Who can resist the smell of lemon, its fresh citrus scent wafting through the air? Once you smell it, you can't be anything but bright and cheery. Many people believe that this scent, standing alone is the perfect aroma for any kitchen.

As a stand-alone fragrance, lemon is a great way to help de-stress you. But beyond that, some scientific studies show that the tart waft of this citrus fruit can actually help boost your immune system. Keep these abilities of lemon in mind when you're making soap for someone who is dealing with stress or seems to catch every cold that passes through.

It's also the perfect complement to . . . well, just about any other essential oil scent you can imagine . . . and especially other citrus aromas.

CEDARWOOD

Here is another essential oil that runs the gambit of varieties of scents, from woody and sweet to dry and smoky. Technically, not all of the cedar wood essential oils you may encounter actually are derived from this plant. The juniper plant has an aroma close to this.

Don't be afraid to check out juniper as well. Whatever ones you decide on, you'll be most pleased.

And you can confidently blend this essential oil with citrus aromas as well sage, rosemary, and lavender.

DARK PATCHOULI

If you've never heard of this as an herb or an essential oil, don't worry. Many people haven't. I know I hadn't until I started soap-making. Despite its musky scent, dark patchouli is actually a member of the mint family and is often used in handcrafted soaps.

This is a calming scent and is often used by people as they meditate.

You may also want to try blending this aroma with any citrus essential oil as well with lavender, sage, or rosemary. Why not see what it does when you combine it with the scent of cinnamon or clove? You may be pleasantly surprised.

ORANGE ESSENTIAL OIL

You know the aroma of the fruit, orange. The familiar scent wafts through the house, the moment someone peels it. The essential oil smells exactly like this. Sweet and juicy. The key to getting the most out of this scent is to use the sweet orange oil, instead of the bitter.

Sweet orange also blends well with just about any other citrus scent.

If you anything about herbs, may you already know that the scent we identify as peppermint can be grown in several different varieties. They range, as you might expect, from sweet to sharp. Many novice soap-makers usually are at a loss as to how to use it and with what other scents you can use it.

Here are a few suggestions you can start with: bergamot, cedarwood, lavender, lemon, rosemary, tea tree, or any evergreen and woodsy essential oils like pine or fir.

BERGAMOT

This is another essential oil I had never heard of until I began soap-making. Now, I wonder how I could not have known about this amazing citrus secret scent. Yes, bergamot belongs to the citrus family and is, in fact, one of the most delicate plants in that family. It requires not only a specific climate to harvest the best fruit, but a special soil as well.

Bergamot has a soothing effect on the mind and a rejuvenating nature on the skin. Not only that, but it blends well with just about any other oil, especially one where it can contribute a warm, spicy floral wafting.

TEA TREE

This is one of the few essential oils you need to use cautiously. And that's only because it's not a fragrance everyone agrees they like. It tends to have a sharp, medicinal smell. The scent some say smells much like camphor.

What would you blend with tea tree? Well, any minty, herbal, minty aromas. Specifically, you may want to blend this with such familiar and refreshing scents as sage, lavender, lemon, and rosemary.

I'm betting this is the first time you've heard of this essential oil. And, yes, that's exactly why I'm including it. It's far too easy to overlook or ignore because it doesn't have a "history" with you. That's okay. I'm here to ask you to give it a chance. I don't believe you'll be disappointed.

What is it? You may know it better as chang, with a tremendously beautiful citrus aroma. If you've never worked with it before you're in for a real treat. While the aroma is citrus, it's a much more well-rounded type of citrus, which makes it perfect in including in soaps. And as for blending it with another, it works best with other citrus aromas.

ESSENTIAL OIL BLENDS

You're sitting at the kitchen table a dozen or so essential oils bottles strewn in front of you. You felt so confident when you bought them. You had plans to mix lemon with... ah...what was that?

No matter you know you'll mix peppermint with . . oops . . .

It sounded so easy when you were reading about these oils, and you were as excited as you were scooping them up at the craft store (you were so excited you couldn't even wait for two-day shipping).

Now, all you have sitting in front of you are ten or twelve separate essential oils and a fear you'll make a batch of soap that smells like . . . well you get the idea.

Don't worry. I've been exactly where you are at the moment. That's why I've included some of my favorite blends of the essential oils I've listed above. Some of these are my creation – feel free to use them.

Some of them I've collected from friends. Some of them were even suggestions from family members after sitting down with me and taking part in an afternoon smell-a-thon. All of them make wonderful scents and fragrances for soaps.

Go, ahead. Try as many of them out as you care. Soon, you'll have a couple of go-to blends. And before you know it you'll be blending your own customized scents.

Here's a hint: When you're ready to blend your own, try only two essential oils, using them on a one to one ratio. That means for every drop (or however you decide to measure your oils) of one, use one drop of the other.

These are a few of my favorite blends!

LEMON BALANCE BLEND

50% Lemon
30% Rosemary
10% Cedarwood
10% Litsea Cubeba

REFRESHING LAVENDER-PEPPERMINT FUSION

35% Peppermint

35% Lavender

20% Patchouli

10% Tea Tree

OCEAN BREEZE

40% Tea Tree

30% Bergamot

20% Orange

10% Litsea Cubeba

OTHER NATURAL INGREDIENTS ADDING CHART

Below is a short chart with a few more natural ingredients you can add to your soap for variety of effects. The variety in this short table is amazing and if you try to use them all, you'll be busy for quite a while. And no doubt you'll love every minute of it.

Natural Addition	How It Works
Almond Oil	Heals irritated skin. Can be used as a base. Possesses a slight odor.
Aloe Vera	Relieves dry skin. Help burned skin heal faster. You can use either in its natural plant form or as a gel.
Apricot	Natural skin softener. Apricot is a popular additive found in many bath products. Put dried fruit in water and soak for several hours before liquefying it.
Apricot Kernel Oil	Softens skin. It's especially effective on sensitive skin.
Beeswax	Helps to harden your soap and provides a calming scent to the bar. Before you add it to your soap, you'll need to melt it. It' not recommended that you use more than one ounce of beeswax for each pound of soap.
Clay	This may seem like a strange addition to soap, but it's great for

	anyone suffering from oily skin. Clay dries out your skin. Your best choice is finely powdered French clay.
Cocoa butter	Not only hardens soap base, but moisturizes your skin. Surprisingly, it looks and smells like white chocolate. If the scent bothers you, purchase it in the scentless variety.
Cucumber	Works as an astringent. Either liquefy the cucumber or merely use the grated skin.
Glycerin	Skin moisturizer
Herbs	Adds colors and textures to your soap.
Honey	Softens soap and moisturizes skin.
Lanolin	Hardens your soap and softens and moisturizes the skin. Should not be used by those are allergic to wool.
Lemon	Contributes to the soap's overall texture and speckles it. Use the grated peel of the fruit. Lemons are also known for their antibacterial

	qualities.
Oatmeal	Adds texture to your soap. In addition, it softens and exfoliates skin. For best results in use, no more than half a cup rolled or one quarter cup ground or pulverized oats for every pound of soap. A blender is a perfect appliance for grinding oats.
Pumice	While pumice is effective at removing tough dirt, its effects can be harsh on the skin. It does, however, add texture to your soap.
Vitamin E oil	The perfect preservative when you have fresh fruit in your soap.
Wheat germ	A great skin exfoliator. It also adds texture and bulk to your soap, while contributing a light speckling to the finished product. Use a maximum of three tablespoons of wheat germ for every pound of soap.

You get the idea by now, I'm sure. Just about anything can be added to your soap creations. And by doing so, you're building your own style – creating your own brand, if you will. If nothing else, you're thoroughly enjoying yourself, and your friends are happy to receive their gifts.

Just remember that the only thing stopping you from trying a new addition in your soap is your own hesitancy.   After you've made a few batches you'll soon discover a "botched batch" is nothing to get upset over and your rate of experimentation will skyrocket.

In the meantime, you may want to try a few of my favorite recipes. They've served me well over the years. Feel free to use any or all of them – and if you like, make any changes to suit your own needs.

Very Berry Mint Soap

Exfoliating Soap for dry skin

Ingredients:

9 oz. suspension melt & pour base

3/4 tsp. 250 IU vitamin E oil

1/4 tsp. raspberry seeds

1/4 tsp. blueberry seeds

Raspberry essential oil

Blueberry essential oil

Peppermint essential oil

FD&C dye (green)

Instructions:

Melt your base soap either in a double boiler or the microwave, whichever one you feel more comfortable using.

Remove this from the heat as soon as it's melted. Stir in the vitamin E oil and add the essential oil to your liking.

Add, one eye dropper at a time, the dye until the soap is a light green color.

Mix the berry seeds in carefully. Then you can pour it into your molds and allow it to harden.

THE SOAP OF MILK AND HONEY

Best used for moisturizing and healing

INGREDIENTS:

2 Tablespoons Olive Oil

2 Tablespoons Water

2 Tablespoons Milk Powder

2 Tablespoons Honey, natural not powdered

Honey, Spice or Vanilla Fragrance Oil if desired

1/2 cup melted Melt and Pour base

INSTRUCTIONS:

Melt your soap according to your preference. When the base is melted, gently stir these ingredients into the soap. Mix thoroughly. Pour this into your molds.

You'll notice that there is no coloring in this recipe. I do this purposely since this soap is created to be a healing agent. You'll discover it'll have a naturally brown color due to the inclusion of the honey. You can use either a white or clear base soap with this. Both will look awesome and provide the necessary healing of the skin.

FLOWER AND HERBAL SOAP

In this particular recipe, I used roses and a few other flowers and herbs which I included in the step by step directions but not the ingredient list. I left that purposefully vague, so when your imagination steps into gear (and it will) you can fill these holes in with ease)

Block of soap base, available at most craft stores
Essential oils
Dried flowers, herbs, spices, and leaves
Soap molds – small cups or trays in various sizes (silicone works best)

I used dried hibiscus, which will turn blue when used, don't panic and rose petals. In addition, I used green tea, and the following herbs all dried: eucalyptus, juniper berries, and rosemary. I also added a bit of dried lemon peel to this as well.

You'll probably want to cut the soap base into cubes so they can melt faster. You can use either a double boiler or a microwave. Again, I can't express how much I prefer the double boiler, but I know many people who swear by the microwave.

Add the essential oil blend to the melted base soap. You'll want to use between five to ten drops of the oils for every ounce of soap you use. Stir this into the melted soap slowly and very gently to prevent any type of bubbles.

Now, go to the molds and arrange your petals, herbs and leaves in them. Once you're satisfied with the placement of these, you can pour your soap into the molds.

Allow this to sit for about an hour. Once the soap is hardened, you can pop them out of the mold.

COFFEE SOAP

What? You've never heard of coffee soap?

To be truthful, I hadn't either until I stumbled on this recipe. It uses not only vanilla essential oil but coffee essential oil. Yes, there really is an essential oil with the amazing fragrance. Who knew?

This, believe it or not, helps to work on reducing that stubborn cellulite. I use it, but because it may offend someone, I don't give it out as a gift. It's not something everyone thinks they need.

Of course, you can conveniently forget to mention the soap's ability to help with cellulite. You'd be surprised how many of your coffee-loving friends would find this quite satisfying.

If you ever find yourself behind a craft table selling your soap, this might be one of your best sellers.

I hope you like it even half as much as I do.

INGREDIENTS:

8 oz. coconut opaque soap base

2 tsp. lanolin

2 tsp. aloe Vera gel

3 tsp. coffee grounds

2 tsp. heavy whipping cream

10 drops essential coffee oil

10 drops vanilla essential oil

INSTRUCTIONS:

Cut the soap base into cubes of similar size, to facilitate the melting. Place these cubes either in a double boiler or a microwave oven, whichever you prefer.

Now add all the ingredients into the melted soap slowly and stir gently. Try not to create bubbles.

Pour this into molds of your choice and allow it to cool. Once it has, you can release the soap from the molds.

VANILLA HONEY OATMEAL RECIPE

Soothing and moisturizing

INGREDIENTS:

2lbs of clear or white melt and pour soap

1/8 to 1/4 cup of Honey

3/4 cup of ground oatmeal

1 tsp of vitamin E

1 tablespoon of Vanilla oil

1 tablespoon of Frankincense and Myrrh oil (Fragrance oil or Essential oil)

INSTRUCTIONS:

Cut the soap base into similar size chunks to make the melting go a bit easier.

The first ingredients you'll add to the melted soap is the honey, and the vitamin E. Allow the base to cool for five to ten minutes. You're looking for skin to form on the top. Stir the skin back into the cooling base. As it begins to thicken you can add the fragrance and oatmeal.

Ideally, you'd like to have the oatmeal suspended in your base.

Once you've done this, pour into your chosen molds. I personally use a loaf pan. I allow it to sit and harden for at least several hours. Any time after that, you can take the soap out of the mold. But, let it sit overnight before you wrap it in plastic wrap.

CHOCOLATE CHIP COOKIE SOAP RECIPE

Soap that looks like cookies! These are perfect for children as well as those who are young at heart. These make great gifts for any holiday or for no reason at all. And yes, by all means, if you attend craft shows selling your soap, take some of these. These are among my best selling soaps.

Once you've completed making this soap, you'll be proud to give a "batch of chocolate chip cookies" to your friends and family. The cocoa butter and powder lend the soap it realistic aroma. Not only that but when you go to wash it, you'll discover you have amazing brown suds.

INGREDIENTS:

1 lb. white or clear coconut soap base
Cocoa powder or brown pigment
1 lb. cocoa butter
1 T chocolate fragrance oil
Small round soap molds

INSTRUCTIONS:

Take the majority of your clear or white soap base, and melt it with the cocoa butter. You'll want to set aside a portion of the soap for later. If you use a white base, I think you'll be very pleased with the shade of brown you'll end up with. It's a great soft brown that looks a lot like a cookie.

Keep this melted, allowing to cool only slightly. As it begins to cool, then you can add the essential chocolate oil.

Now take the soap you didn't melt, and melt that now. Once it's melted, add the dark brown dye or a cocoa powder. You're looking for a much deeper brown than that of the rest of the soap. Hint: this will become your chocolate chips.

Pour the smaller, darker portion of the soap over a waxed paper lined plate and allow it to dry until it just gets to that tacky stage. Observe this carefully, because it won't take long to occur. At this point, you'll want to break off several chunks which will be your chocolate chips, and you'll line them at the bottom of the molds.

If you'd like you can spritz this with alcohol. At this point, pour the larger portion of the soap base, which should have cooled some, but is still in a semi-liquid state, over your "chips."

Allow this to sit for a while until you get another skin to form on top. At this time you'll add more "chips." This makes the "cookie" look like it has chocolate chips spread throughout it.

If you'd like, you can also add a couple of chips to blend into the rest of the soap, just to make it look even more like a "real" chocolate chip cookie.

CHAPTER 9: 15 COLORING TRICKS THAT WILL SURPRISE YOU

I couldn't resist.

This is a chapter of some tips you can use to help create an even better atmosphere when you're making soap. Some of them will help you perfect pouring out your colors, others will help you avoid either melting the soap too much, or stirring too fast, or even just getting too impatient throughout the process.

I made most of these at one time and if I didn't one of my friends did. I hope you have a great time and also learn from my mistakes. Read through them all at least once. They aren't found in any real order.

You'll discover that you'll read one that you don't believe you'll ever need is probably going to be the first one you'll need to put to use.

SWIRLING COLORS TIPS

1. The most important thing you need to know about creating color swirls in melt and pour soap can be accomplished, as long as you make sure the base soap is already cooling. If you pour your second color – the color you want to swirl through your base – when the base is too warm you won't get a swirl. The second color will get lost and mixed with the base color.

2. Making concentric circles. Keeping the advice you just read in mind, concentric swirls are easier to make than you think – even in the melt-and-pour method. Take the one or two colors from the swirls and swirl them on top of the soap base. You'll need to work quickly before the base cools

too much. When you pop these out of the molds, you'll see the rings of colors.

3. The thicker the soap when you pour your second color in, the thicker your swirls will be.

4. The warmer the soap that i, the thinner the soap base, the thinner and more delicate that second color that wafts through it will appear.

5. Yes, you can make layers. Just like in working with swirls, the temperature is the key. Make sure the top layer of soap is not too hot, or you guessed it, it will begin to melt the layer on which you're pouring. Melt and pour melts at about 120 degrees Fahrenheit. So when you're layering your soap, be sure to use a thermometer.

6. When you're creating layers of different colors, use powdered pigments and not dyes. The dye is formed from smaller particles than the pigment and will problem bleed into the layers on either side of it. The pigments, however, are formed

using larger particles and won't be soaking into the layer below it.

7. Yes, your soap really does have an "expiration date." You can store your creations for approximately six months. If you don't use it within that time period, it may physically deform and dry out.

8. Before you place your soap in packages for gifts or to sell, be sure it sits out to dry for two days.

9. If you're in a hurry, you can place your not-yet-hardened soap in a refrigerator, but for no longer than 15 minutes. That should help speed the process some.

10. Before you pour your melted soap into the bars, make sure the bars are in a spot that won't be disturbed. It's easier to move soap once it hardens in the molds than try to take the molds with the melted soap someplace else. (Trust me, I learned this one the hard way!)

11.   If you find that your soap is stubbornly clinging to its mold, refusing to release, try spraying your molds with cooking spray before you pour the liquid in, much like you do with your cupcake or cookie trays. Once you spray a bit, take a paper towel to not only remove the excess but to smooth the thin layer out.

12.   Adding embedded objects is easier than it looks. When you pour your soap into the molds, don't fill it to the top as you normally do. Instead, stop partially through then wait for about 10 to 15 minutes. Just enough time to allow the soap to gel. Then place the object in the mold, spritz it with alcohol and then fill the mold the rest of the way with your melted base.

13.   Before you do your final scent check of your soap, sniff some coffee. Yes, it sounds strange, but by doing so, you'll be clearing your nose of all other scents. This will allow you to get a true aroma of what you've put in your soap.

14.	After a while, you'll know how much soap you'll need to fill a mold just by "eyeing" it – when you first start so, not so much. An easy way to "guesstimate" the amount of melted soap is simple enough. Fill the mold with water, then pour it into a measuring cup. This is about the amount you'll need. But use a little more soap than you measured, you'll undoubtedly have some soap base stick to the sides of the melting container.

15.	Looking for natural pigments as well as natural exfoliates? Think ground spices. That's right. Try ground cinnamon or nutmeg. These two spices will give your soap a nice shade of browns and beiges. If you're searching for some earthy orange and yellow shades, try putting turmeric and paprika in your soap. The coarser the spice you add, you'll discover the more it'll act like an exfoliate for your skin.

So you're thinking about taking your hobby to the next level and perhaps starting a part-time business making soap and selling it locally and online. But you just don't know it's feasible.

How much soap would you need to make? In order to make a profit? Or is it even possible to make a profit considering what's involved? And how much would you charge, anyway? And whatever the prices is, how can you be sure people would pay that much for the soap.

All Legitimate Concerns.

What if I told you that it's possible in a single workday you can, with enough practice, make a hundred bars of soap from the initial melting to the final wrapping of the product?

Don't dismiss this out of hand or take this as the smug bragging of someone who is having the time of her life with her own profitable soap-making business.

CONSIDER THESE STATISTICS.

With practice, you could easily melt and pour enough soap into bar molds that will eventually yield 100 bars in a mere two hours.

After it has dried for several days, you can carve this batch of bar soap into 100 bars. This should take you about two hours, once you've been working with soap long enough.

Then, all that's left to do is to wrap these 100 bars in an attractive manner.

Once you get your own personal "conveyor belt" of soap products moving, you'll discover that you won't have any time lag in the hardening. Make bars every day and there'll always be some soap ready to be cut. So in a mere six hours in a day, you have 100 bars to sell.

Then there's the question of what you charge for them.

Knowing that prices fluctuate from region to region, your costs for these supplies could vary, but overall you're looking at a bar that cost you no more than a dollar. If you've been to craft fairs and priced soap, you're probably well aware that the bar soap is selling for about $5 a bar.

Wow! That means that the ***potential profit*** in one bar is $4 and on that modest batch of 100 is $400. There is a potential to create an income-generating business.

I can offer you guidelines and suggestions on launching your soap-making business, but there's one thing you must eventually decide for yourself; is it the business for you, your family and your lifestyle?

With an eye to that question, here are just a few of the advantages of a cottage soap-making business:

The start-up costs are modest.

Look around you. Carefully review what it would cost to get your business started and giving off an air of professionalism at the same time.

The supplies you'll need are easily found.

In fact, you have a great start because you already have the soap supplies. It's only a matter of finding the supplies that would take you to that next level.

The equipment you'll need is minimal and easily obtained.

 As with the supplies, you have just about everything you'll need to start your business right now. Any additional investment can be small, changing some of your equipment as you can afford it.

Making soap is relatively easy and can be learned quickly.

You've already had a jump start on the essential knowledge of this craft. You may want to add a few more techniques to what you know to widen your breadth of potential sales. But you've got the basics practically mastered right now.

There's a built-in niche market of potential buyers.

All you need to do is tour a craft festival. Every person attending is a potential buyer. Homemade soap is something that not only would a consumer buy for herself but would be glad to snatch up around the holidays as quick and easy holiday gifts.

From gift exchanges to giving the unexpected visitor during the holidays a little something, there are a myriad of reasons why people would buy it.

There are seemingly an infinite number of ways you can set your product apart from others and create a demand for it.

From scents to colors to a wide variety of embedded items, you can pride yourself on the fact that probably no two items are ever exactly alike.

You can also effortlessly create accessory products to sell along with your soap.

As we've already seen, these are a potential for profit.

There are any number of venues at which you can sell your products.

You can be as busy as you want, from working weekends only, to selling at local and regional swap meets and flea markets during the week. In fact, once you get into a rhythm you could be busy a couple hours a day.

Some days you would stay home and create and the other days schedule yourself at craft events and flea markets. And that doesn't even include the online sales potential.

6 STEPS BEFORE STARTING YOUR BUSINESS

Here are the steps every soap maker takes when she's moving from hobbyist to business person. These steps are, of course, a quick overview, but it does give you something to think about in general terms.

1. Decide what your "most popular" soap gifts are? What do your friends and family like the best.

2. These are probably going to be the core of your inventory. Think about building your business around these.

3. Visit events where others are selling their soaps.

See what type of potential buyers there are for these products and see if the "competition" sells the same ones you make.

Don't be afraid to ask the seller what his best sellers are. You don't need to him you're thinking about starting your own business. This will give you some idea of what some customers want.

4. Use friends and family members as focus groups.

Show them what you're thinking of selling and the prices. Once you get their opinions, give them gifts of your soap so they can provide feedback. Take notice of what they choose. These items may be your best sellers.

5. Compose an email list for future orders

Eventually, everyone who makes soap has to come to the realization that the product will eventually be washed down the drain. And that's a good thing.

That means there is the potential for re-orders. And here is where you can not only make more money but ensure the security of your business.
Follow up on those who either took gifts or bought soap.

6. Use Social Media to your advantage

Nowadays, social media is one of the most powerful marketing and selling tools that is available for free. You should really take advantage of these new platforms. They are free to use and most importantly since you most likely already are on Facebook.

Start with the simple one, like Facebook, let all your friends and family know what you are up to and offer all of them a hefty discount to try out your products.

Create a Facebook fan page or a Facebook group, ask them to join in where you only discuss anything and everything under the sun about you new found hobby of soap crafting.

Once you master Facebook, then move on to other platforms like Instagram, Twitter and others.

4 STEPS TO OPENING YOUR HOME-BASED SOAP BUSINESS

BRAND YOUR BUSINESS

Branding your business more than just picking up colors or logo, it is what will identify your business to the customers. It is the total package, your logo, your brand's name, your soap's unique color, packaging or color, all together makes a brand.

So be careful when choosing a name or the logo as they need to go hand in hand, they need to scream the words QUALITY SOAP. Once you create a brand successfully, you can then move on to the next step.

I personally didn't have much money, so I went to Fiverr.com and paid $5 each to get two different logo designs and then picked one. It is a website where you can hire various talents from around the world for $5 /task. Impressive, huh?

Once I did that, I also found someone on that site who for $5 offered 20 plus catchy names for my brand, again I picked one of those names. And, lastly, again I went on Fiverr and hired a graphic designer to design some attractive packaging for me, and in just two days I had two different designs to pick from. So for less than $50, I had all three tasks done, and I am sure you can too.

EFFECTIVE PRICING STRATEGY

After branding, you do need to look deep into pricing, and how you should price your products. For this, you need some serious market research, and when I say market research, find out who else is making soaps in your area, what their quality is and how they differ from your soaps. Then find out how much they are selling for.

Once you know these details, sit down, figure out how your product, packaging and color or fragrance differs or compares to theirs.

Once you analyze all that data, carefully price your product accordingly, but do remember not to price yourself out of the market just because you think your soap is one of a kind and no one in the world has made such soaps.

LICENSING AND REGULATIONS

For you to have a successful business even if it a home-based one, there are specific steps you will have to take.

For example, regardless of state, you will have to have the followings

A. File your articles of incorporation with the Secretary of State of your own State unless you want to be identified as a sole proprietor.
B. Apply for all 3 (City, County, and State) business licenses which you can do at the city hall office

C. Talk to an accountant to find out if you need to file and obtain an EIN)Employer Identification number) from the IRS, if you are a sole proprietor, then your social security number will act as your EIN number

D. Comply with FDA, Consumer product safety commission, and FTC in the event if your soaps have claims such as "moisturizing," "Cleanser" or any such claims.

Here are the websites for all three agencies so you can read and check for yourself to see if you need to comply with any of their requirements.

https://www.fda.gov/Cosmetics/GuidanceRegulation/default.htm

https://www.cpsc.gov/Regulations-Laws--Standards/Unregulated-Products/

https://www.ftc.gov/enforcement/rules/rulemaking-regulatory-reform-proceedings/fair-packaging-labeling-act

In the event you live in Florida and California, where they impose stricter laws, you do need to check with these websites below to make sure you are complying with all of their requirements.

For Florida go here.

http://www.myfloridalicense.com/dbpr/ddc/CosmeticManufactu
rer.html

For California go here.

https://www.cdph.ca.gov/Pages/PageNotFoundError.aspx?requ
estUrl=https://www.cdph.ca.gov/programs/cosmetics/Pages/d
efault.aspx

MARKETING

Essentially marketing is what makes or breaks a
product and its chance for success or even failure.
Regardless, if you make the best soaps in the world,
without proper and effective marketing, no one will
know about your soaps. So plan a simple but effective
marketing campaign that produces fruit.

For this, you don't have to spend a lot of money or
have a huge budget. Most of the marketing can be
done for free. Here are some steps you can take to
start your marketing campaign.

A. Use social media (as I just mentioned earlier)
B. Market in local craft stores
C. Set up a booth at local Flea market

D. Arrange home parties where you display soaps and gift baskets to your friends and family
E. Local churches
F. Local social events
G. Local schools

SELLING SOAP WHEN MARKETING ISN'T YOUR AREA OF EXPERTISE

Let's face it. Few of us are born marketers. Even fewer of us have ever had to think about marketing any product, let alone home-made soap, seriously. So, it's natural for you to tread lightly into the idea of launching your own business

A large aspect of customized soap products is to simply tell your own story. The odds are after that, the products will then practically sell themselves. By that I mean when you strike up a conversation with a potential customer, you can talk about what prompted you to start your hobby and how it eventually turned into a business.

It could be that your concern over the potentially dangerous additives in commercially made soap triggered your business. Or the realization that people were eager to buy moderately priced gifts that looked impressive for holidays and birthdays.

While you are doing all of this "chit-chatting", you're also learning the first rule of sales. People are far more likely to buy a product from someone they consider a friend than a stranger.

And while you're doing this, if you realize or not, you're dissolving your doubts and fears about your lack of marketing skills.

If you're at a craft show, consider displaying a photo album of you making the soap. You could even show them how step by step it starts as a liquid to a beautiful bar of soap.

One of the advantages of selling soap is that the soap speaks for itself. It's hard to resist an attractively packaged product like soap that's moderately priced.

If you'd like you can even dig in and capture a niche within this market itself. Think organic, for example. The American consumer is more adamant about buying organic than at any other time in recent years.

Organic soap would fall right into this niche and not only will your business attract those who love homemade soap, but those who want to purchase as many organic products as possible.

And when you do this, guess what? You're beginning to brand your business. The next thing you know, you're business will gain a reputation as "Natural and Organic soap."

You can do this with any ingredient in your soaps. Perhaps you're known for your unique incredible blend of essential oils. There you have it. You've set yourself apart from the other soap businesses.

CONCLUSION

Excited about starting your melt-and-pour adventure?

What? You started making soap even before you finished reading this book?

I shouldn't be surprised. I would be doing the same thing. And if you're anything like me, you're probably already hooked on the hobby.

Making soap is a fun and useful gift. And perhaps it's those two qualities of it that makes it so much fun to make and to sell. Making soap can become a family affair – or an activity you covet when everyone else is out of the house.

I sincerely hope this short guide has helped you even a bit. I believe I've covered everything you'll need to know to get well on your way to providing your family and friends with not only delightful gifts for every holiday, but also with some sensationally healthy ones at that.

One of the things I'm the proudest of when I make soap aren't the colors I used, but avoiding coming into contact with potential health damaging additives. And the rest is just the icing on the cake.

Mmm . . . Excuse me. That just reminded me I wanted to make soap that looked like cupcakes. Boy, this is going to be fun.

LAST WORDS

I want to say THANK YOU for purchasing and reading this book. I really hope you got a lot out of it!

I am neither a professional writer nor an author, but rather a person who always had the passion for making and crafting beautiful soaps and since I have been making soaps for last 15 years now, I figured it is about time I share my knowledge with you, as I know there are many people who share the same passion and drive as I do.

Despite my best effort to make this book error free, if you happen to find any errors, I want to ask for your forgiveness ahead of time.

Just remember, my writing skills may not be best, but the knowledge I share here is pure and honest.

Can I ask you for a quick favor though?

If you enjoyed this book, I would really appreciate it if you could leave me a Review on Amazon.

I LOVE getting feedback from my wonderful readers, and reviews on Amazon really do make the difference.

I read all of my reviews and would love to hear your thoughts. If you rather give me a direct feedback feel free to email me at MollyBarrett2017@gmail.com Thank you so much!!

Molly Barrett

Printed in Great Britain
by Amazon

20467019R20088